The Hundred-Year House

WINDFALL POETRY SERIES

The Hundred-Year House

Poems by

Michael McDowell

Windfall Press
Portland, Oregon

Acknowledgements: Thanks to the following publications where
some of the poems in this book first appeared:
   Alchemy Magazine of Literature and Art
   Alchemy Chapbook Series No. 4
   The Bridge
   Confluence: A Portland Anthology
   Northwind Anthology 2008
   Walking Bridges Using Poetry as a Compass
   Windfall: A Journal of Poetry of Place

Cover art: *Long Beach Laundry*, by LaVonne Tarbox Crone
Watercolor • 11 x 14 inches • 1998
www.tarboxcrone.com

Cover and text design: Cheryl McLean

Windfall Press
PO Box 19007
Portland, OR 97280-0007
www.windfalljournal.com

McDowell, Michael J. 1951–
   The hundred-year house: poems / Michael McDowell
Library of Congress Control Number: 2011938770
ISBN: 978-0-9700302-2-1

For Janis, Andrew, Julia

I have travelled a good deal in Concord.

—Henry David Thoreau

Contents

I. Beach

II. City

III. Mountains

I. Beach

Ocian in view! O! the joy.

—William Clark,
Journals of Lewis & Clark,
7 November 1805

Sand in the Sheets

My father had no use for the beach.
He complained of sand in his shoes,
of overcast and fog and run-down houses,
and at night of sand between the sheets.

He liked the beach best with sun on his back,
looking down the fairway of his imagination
from a golf course tee in summertime Portland
with a wood in hand and sand confined to traps.

Yet most Fridays each summer he'd leave Portland to drive
for hours on single-lane highways of slow-moving cars
through mountains and tidal plains and onto the ferry
to join his wife and kids for two days and nights.

With his wife he walked the beach and ate sand in his food
and, while my siblings slept in adjacent beds,
quietly conceived me in the beach house attic
despite sand in the sheets and the fog.

Betsy

Betsy, the driftwood horse swing,
hung by two ropes
from the leaning crabapple
in our Seaview beachhouse lot.

A generation of children climbed into Betsy's saddle
and rode to surf sounds through the Willapa Hills,
heading them off at the pass
somewhere near Beard's Hollow, or Chinook.

Cisco Kid hat, pearl-handled cap guns,
Davy Crockett coonskin cap, cowboy chaps—
all the paraphernalia of violence and
conquest rode beneath that crabapple.

One June when we arrived at the house,
the tree had fallen. My uncle George
had cut up the trunk where it lay. Like a hatcheted snake
it crawled in sections diagonally across the yard.

Betsy was nowhere to be found—maybe burned in the
woodstove, salt-soaked seawood snapping.
We have since learned to ride other, invisible horses
beneath treeless skies.

Burnt Toast

At breakfast the old toasters sat at either end of the table,
one next to the spoon jar and one next to the sugar jar,
chrome-plated steel on yellow oilcloth.

The sides leaned together to make an *A*, like hands praying.
We lowered each side, put in the bread slices,
closed the doors, and watched the coils glow.

Early morning, distracted by woodstove, siblings,
comics, and talk, we'd smell and then see
a pillar of smoke rising from the praying hands,

a sacrifice bumping against the sooty heaven
of the kitchen ceiling, signaling we'd failed
in our vigilance and not opened the doors in time.

Then we'd scrape the black cinders into the sink.
On such occasions my grandfather would say,
"I've always liked my toast a little charred."

So we learned to accept black specks on jellied toast,
like the burnt tapioca and black-bottomed cookies,
expecting no sweetness without ashes in the mouth.

Pine Cones

After the hot oatmeal, our mother sends us forth into the morning fog
to pick up the fallen cones beneath the giant spruce and shore pines.
We earn five cents for every grocery sack of cones.

They last as well as Pres-to-logs in the kitchen woodstove:
After the fury of kindling and the steady flame of larger wood,
the cones pump out heat, each seed in turn throbbing a red glow.

My brothers and sisters spread out across the summertime yard,
hunched like gleaners to harvest our own lawn.
When I stand up, cool ocean mist falls full on my face.

Some cones hide in the woven mat of lawn, grass between the bracts.
Others have settled like saints in their own little pocket catacombs.
Their ghostly white mold glows in the overcast morning.

We fill the sacks like our mother did, and our aunts and uncles,
grateful that spruce, pine, and fir shake all winter
to provide us these cones for our cooking and heat.

We take our full sacks to the woodshed by the garbage pit
and line them up beneath shelves of kerosene lamps and glass chimneys
where they'll dry and open to burn more readily.

A half-dozen new nickels send us pumping our bicycles
through the cool July streets for Popsicles and Creamsicles,
the cold indulgences of summer at Joe Sugarman's store.

Ilwaco Bakery

Once a week in sweatshirts and jeans
we'd drive, not walk, six kids and a mom—to Ilwaco, a city,
with a main street, a movie house, two bakeries,
and a hundred fishing boats in the harbor.

After new canvas shoes at Doupé Brothers'
we'd walk the slippery and skittering docks.
Once my sister stepped between sections
and sank to her shoulders in the murky water.

At the warm bakery we'd get
A half-dozen loaves of uncut sweet Holman bread
and a cream-filled puff pastry for each,
covered with powdered sugar which vaporized at a touch.

The ride back to Seaview we'd discuss how to eat:
the best kind of bite, the appropriate speed of consumption,
the right combination of custard and shell
as our childhood summers slowly vaporized.

Wash Day

Summertime at the beach,
all six kids wore and rewore unwashed clothes,
bike-chain oil growing darker on the pants legs,

pitch from the pine trees like medallions on our shirts.
The odd oatmeal flake and dried-milk patch
set off the weak brown of the sandy peninsula soil

worn like leather patches on our elbows
and knees and bottoms. Our clothing displayed our world,
until wash day.

The old wringer washer sat heavy
on the sloped floor of the addition behind the kitchen.
We cleared away boxes and piled our clothes.

In went t-shirts, jeans, sweatshirts, sheets.
The house shook as the agitator churned
load after load of a gray soup.

The wringer above the tub transformed
soggy shirts and underwear into smooth flat packages
we hand-delivered to siblings in the yard

where a half-dozen clotheslines ran from nails
pounded into house-boards, across the wide lot
to the shore pines along the property line.

We propped the ropes sagging with clothes
with a dozen V-notched sticks
tilting at crazy angles across the yard.

Shirts with tails pinned up and sleeves hanging down
seemed to dive into the sea of our dandelion lawn.
We chased each other through the rooms of bedsheet walls.

The clothes dangled all day under the cloudy sky,
billowing in the ocean breeze and then drooping,
still damp at dinner when we finally pulled them down.

The Long Beach Theater

The Long Beach theater printed a month's worth of movies
in a brochure that opened like our grade-school report cards
listing not grades but movies that changed every three days.

Sometimes after dinner our mother would drop us off,
five siblings, for the current show.
A narrow set of cushioned seats faced forward.
Wallpaper cornstalks towered over us.

After the movie, we'd walk the two miles home
along the beach, heading south.
Away from the town's lights, we were just voices talking in the darkness.
We kept the crashing surf a safe distance to the right
as we walked the wet sand.

After it seemed we should be at Seaview,
we wondered if we'd missed the approach
and were headed towards Beard's Hollow
and the rock wall of North Head jutting into the ocean.

We walked with our arms stretched in front of us
in the pitch darkness, anticipating the sudden basalt,
wondering about broken fingers, bloodied noses and lips.

With arms outstretched like sleepwalkers
or a set of Frankenstein's monsters lurching toward their doom,
we'd stumble on the deeps ruts leading to the Seaview approach,
find the crumbled rocks of its welcome flat bed, and head inland
where we knew to expect a glowing porch light,
a baby brother already asleep,
and the comfort of sand-sprinkled sheets.

Aunt Lippy's House

Tioga, Long Beach, Washington

Late evenings we kids lay outside on our backs.
The crinkly dune grass poked into our t-shirts,
and the warm, damp sky pressed upon us.

An Instamatic flash froze us in Pompeii poses
when my sister photographed five siblings sprawled
in the grass like corpses.

We could hear grown-ups in the house laugh and talk.
On the August dune we watched the stars'
bright linear messages chalked across a blackboard sky.

Then we rose like ghosts and walked
by starlight back to kitchen
card games and ordinary talk.

The Hundred-Year House

1883
At our beach house, my great-grandfather tells jokes
as my great-grandmother walks the property line
with pine seeds in her apron and a child in her arm,
planting carefully every ten feet in the sandy soil.

1918
Over by the salal my grandmother pumps water into a pan
which her daughter has set on pine needles and moss
and talks of running a pipe to the kitchen.

1925
Her son Tod, dead these seventy years, struggles with the push-mower
against the too-tall beach grass beneath the shore pines.
After a pitchy climb, he can see twenty miles out to sea.

1929
My mother sits on the summer porch in darkness with her sister and cousir
talking of the evening's dance and the local boys
and the boys they'll return to in the city.

1960
Burnt-sugar smells of the late-night taffy pull
still linger on the rambling front porch,
sticky-sweet laughter hardening into candy.

Silhouetted in the late afternoon sun
my teenage cousins Terry and Robbie leap in the surf,
the enthusiasm of adolescence and wealth combined.
Their older sister Carolyn, golden, rises from the waves.

2000

My daughter giggles at the book she's reading,
the clock gongs the half-hour, and the rain gurgles in the drain-pipes
above the dry August yard.

She will fall asleep watching North Head Light wink in 20 seconds, then 10,
through pines and over the dunes beyond the butte,
her eyes locked on the promise of stories
about that salal, those fishing rocks, that spruce, this beach.

Memorial Day Weekend

A canvas bag of final papers awaits comments and grades,
but I bicycle up and down the dunes instead and through the shore pines
where olive-sided flycatchers whistle "Seaview! Seaview!"
and past red-winged blackbirds yodeling in the froggy marsh.

At North Head the overcast mutes an almost-summer sun.
On the cliffs around the rusting lighthouse
fresh-leafed cow-parsnips offer plates of white delicacies
high above the blue tablecloth of ocean.

I lean on the handlebars, my tire chewing at the edge of the bluff.
The combers below break and move stately toward shore,
each leading wave spreading its field of foam
like so many unread pages of student papers.

It's almost the time of long bike rides,
endless pleasure-reading, swimsuits, evening beach fires.
I want to be this ladybug on a buttery blossom of Scotch broom,
or that bald eagle floating like a summer afternoon, above pestering gulls.

But ink, not ocean, is my liquid for now, which I send scrawling
across those white deserts of crumpled sentences
where a rare idea ventures into a risky ocean like a new jetty
from which I can see bright sun on a white hull, at a distance of about two
 weeks.

Waiting for Janis

Twilit Long Beach from Pro Video to Seaview,
weekend tourists have multiplied on the sidewalks.
Swollen minivans and RVs drop litters of
kids and sweatshirted spouses on sidestreets.

The children and I await your arrival from the city.
Dinner's put away and dishes washed,
the fireplace snaps and cracks the fallen pine,
and new "Welcome!" cards sit on the table.

Without you, our meals have missed their seasoning,
our beach walks have missed your hands,
and the bed is just a bed,
the night just the darkness until morning.

With you here, the anemones and starfish return to the tide pools,
the ocean again booms and roars in the distance,
the coastal tidelands envelope us with their scents,
the moon rises full through the shore pines and spruce.

Senator Corbett's Pasture

Senator Corbett's pasture has disappeared behind a new garage.
From our kitchen sink we see only slats and shingles
and tops of trees against the low coastal clouds.

Senator Corbett's pasture used to graze cows.
From the dusty street we watched them munch
as we walked, nickels in hand, to Sugarman's Store.

Senator Corbett's pasture long ago used to graze chestnut horses,
when his family and servants summered
on this peninsula of pines and brown pelicans.

Now Senator Corbett's pasture grazes RVs parked side by side.
Super-sized families in t-shirts and caps
hose dead fish on the grass beneath the awnings.

We hear their scooters buzz the length of the pasture,
behind the slats and shingles of the new cedar garage,
where once the cows and horses stood in coastal fog.

Coastal Forest Mosquitoes

Cape Disappointment

On our arms and legs constellations form
unique as freckle patterns,
each bite our donation of blood
to the next generation of larvae.

On the Baker Bay trail the bites multiply as fast as
we pull the red huckleberries into our metal cups.
My daughter wears nubs of horns on her forehead,
two rounded buttes rising east and west.

At McKenzie Head mosquitoes as big as Anna's hummingbirds
hover by neck and cheek and hand.
My son has itched and scratched and rubbed
his legs into ranges of red-cratered volcanoes.

So we enter the landscape,
leaving our blood living in others,
our human cells flying past sitka and salmonberry
to places we'd never go.

At evening on the porch
as we count and compare our new coins of raised flesh,
mosquitoes wing from the wax myrtles and pines
to our waiting arms and legs.

North Head Batteries

Mouth of the Columbia

Fort Columbia, Fort Canby, Fort Stevens—
long ago the military poured concrete
bunkers and batteries and lookouts
for an enemy that never arrived.

My family walks the bluffs and into the bunkers.
We climb into the giant concrete skulls whose
eye slits forever watch the Pacific horizon.

Gun mounts sprout from the floor,
steel support beams and doors and brackets
flake a century of rust like old-growth bark.

Julia climbs out the window like an ant
out an eye socket. Our springer spaniel rests
head on paws in the grass on bunker top: a fur hat.

I rummage through debris, kicking
around wartime thoughts:
Cruise missiles and IEDs now explode daily

while here, wind and rain,
surf and sun, and all creation work
to decay the materiel of war.

Dozens of Brandt's cormorants
congregate and strut the rocks below.
Bronze sea lions haul out to sun.

Mudflats

At morning low tide we walk onto the Willapa mudflats.
The slick hummocks near shore give way
to rich black muck which sucks off my sneakers, my daughter's
flip-flops, her friend's boots. We struggle until we reach
the firmer, siltier mud under a few inches of water.

A half mile from shore, the turning tide sways eelgrass.
We flex our fingers into the mud searching
for the hard lumps of Pacific littlenecks and manilas,
looking for life beneath the visible world.
We have guests at the house to feed tonight.

Fog obscures the far shore, five miles distant.
An island's treeline stands a darker gray.
In every direction gray mutes the flat, wet world.
We stoop as we slosh through the cold water,
grasping and plunking hardshells into our buckets.

Medieval pilgrims walked mudflats,
coming from throughout Europe
to the Benedictine abbey of Mont St. Michel
on its granite island in a silty French bay
looking not for clams, but grace.

The tides rushed in across those flats
à la vitesse d'un cheval au gallop, at the speed of a horse in gallop,
and the unlucky few who'd miscalculated distance and tide,
or lost their bearings in fog and gray, stood mired in quicksand
crying to the saints for rescue until swirling water rose above their heads.

I call the girls with their orange and neon-green buckets.
The buckets brim with tight-lipped clams trailing wisps of grass.
My daughter estimates our take. The water now swirls
calf-high. As we head to shore, the faint sun reaches
through the haze to dry our hands and warm our backs.

Seaview Beach Approach, August Afternoons

The crumbly rock of the approach
sinks into the drying sand. Vehicle after vehicle
reaches the western edge of the continent
and rolls from the last road onto a wet-sand beach.

As the vehicles race the surf-line past kids and gulls
we lean on a driftwood log, counting the crab boats
and observing the sand ruts
grow deeper with each car and truck.

At last one SUV
sinks to its axle, guns its engine,
spews rooster tails of dry sand,
and sinks even deeper.

Everyone applauds
and no one helps
till another vehicle arrives
and the men get out and stand around

and point here and there and
look for driftwood planks or boards
and someone pulls out a rope or a chain,
someone else a shovel.

The curling waves sparkle like polished green marble.
The ocean's roar erases shouts and gunned engines.
The men dig and pull against the backdrop of foaming surf,
their backs to the water and dull roar.

It's best when the tide is coming in
and the leading waves bounce over dry sand castles and footprints
to creep closer to the doomed truck.
The men eventually notice, and point, and run around faster.

They jump up and down on the bumper
till eventually a man slips and falls back,
a rope or chain pulls taut, and the rocking SUV bursts free of the sand
and hits the bumper of the pulling truck.

The men slap each other's backs,
scribble on pieces of paper which they exchange,
and the vehicles spew gravel and exhaust at the ocean
as they race up the approach toward town and its two taverns.

We listen to the ocean's unceasing complaint
as the smallest waves begin to cover the digging.
Gulls and brown pelicans settle and then circle,
and the afternoon sparkles on the swells.

The Drownings This Summer

The drownings this summer
float beneath the conversations,
surfacing at four o'clock cocktails.

That Spanaway boy, Helen says, leaning in her chair.
Eighteen, high school basketball star,
as strong and fit as anyone could be.

His friends told the reporters he just went out too far.
They knelt at surf's edge and watched the waves
for the body to return.

We watched and heard the Jayhawk copter,
motor lifeboat, jet skis skim the surface,
even at midnight working an invisible grid.

At sunrise Saturday, his friends found the body
floating near the Bolstad approach,
the ocean having done what it does:

The rip current sucks swimmers beyond the break line
while they struggle against the current, till
fatigue and hypothermia still the arms and legs.

Yet every day I take my daughter and her friend into the ocean,
where in wetsuits and leashed to boogie boards
we ride the waves in.

Let's do "dead woman floating," the girls laugh.
They lie face-down in the water, their long hair floating
while the waves toss them round and round and I worry

until a minute later they rise and stand beaming in delight,
wetsuits deep black and glistening like harbor seals,
born again into life on solid ground.

How to Drown

The searcher says that the drowned
typically lie on their backs,
their arms reaching up
and waving gently in the currents.

On sonar, the image is of a W,
the dead near the end of the alphabet
with their bodies beginning one last word:
Wait! Why? What's up?

Drowning's not difficult, he says.
All it takes is one gasp
at the icy surprise of the water's sudden hug
and it's in the mouth, throughout the lungs,

dissolving the oily film on lung sacs
so they can't do their work
of moving oxygen into blood cells:
water balloons sag heavy in the chest.

Then it's time to leave, with so much unsaid.
Wave those arms goodbye: W, W, W:
Auf Widersehen. Ave atque vale!
When will we walk again with those we've loved?

The 9-point Earthquake and Tsunami

"I don't want to have to fly over this area and find that
everyone's been killed." —Congressman Brian Baird,
about tsunami preparations on the Long Beach Peninsula

There can't be a tsunami now—
dinner's almost ready.
We've just had wireless installed.
The children are only in high school.
The family's vacationed here safely for a hundred years.

OK to the warning sirens,
OK to the hidden emergency caches,
OK to the evacuation route signs,
OK to the detailed elevation maps,
OK to the meetings and plans.

But if there's anything we've learned,
it's to live as if there will be no immediate death and disaster,
as if the seasons will cycle as always,
equinox following solstice,
windstorm following rainstorm, snowstorm, flood.

If there's anything we've learned about how to live,
it's to balance fear with "common sense"
and put what paralyzes us into the far-off future—
earthquake in the Cascadia subduction zone,
liquifaction of this sandy soil, hundred-foot-high tsunamis.

Yes, nature can work swiftly;
life is fragile; towns and civilizations rise and fall.
Now, look at the sun sparkle on the foaming surf,
the wasp entering the purple foxglove—
and here's some garlic butter for tonight's grilled salmon.

Clam Tide

Clamming weekends,
the countryside rises and drives to the coast.

Razor clams know to keep their necks down,
but when the tide goes out
and the sun sets a flatiron of spilled orange juice across the horizon,
then it's hard not to wiggle the digger,
chew a little sand, and
spurt hello to the world in a parabolic arc.

My son and I descend with the rest of the world
onto the October beach.
As far as the eye can see, kids, parents, graybeards
mill about the glistening wet sand with bent heads,
looking for signs of inner life:
a dimple here, a doughnut there.

Clam licenses pinned to shoulders fluttering in the wind,
surf roaring in the background,
we send the sand flying
with clam shovels and clam tubes.

As the clams race deeper faster,
we drop to our knees
and dig the last sloppy foot with our hands,
heads bowed toward the ocean,
the entire wet beach our prayer rug.

Beach Bonfire

After sunset we walked north,
my children pushing bicycles through dry sand,
till we came to driftwood logs and built a fire.

Families flying kites in the twilight packed and left,
the clouds flew off northwest to southwest,
and darkness settled around the flames whipping in the wind.

Because we sang the right songs for this northern beach,
songs my mother's mother taught her,
and told the old stories with our toasted marshmallows,

hundreds of stars came out, the surf crashed louder,
and the lighthouse on North Head three miles away
winked especially for us.

As the bonfire turned to coals,
our water bottles of ocean water with fierce hiss and steam
plunged us into darkness.

My daughter said, "Look, the waves are glowing!"
In the booming black night, every cresting wave's white foam
glowed phosphorescent as a Halloween glowstick.

"It's millions of tiny sea creatures," I said, "each giving off light."
We walked south along the night beach,
patterns of light glowing, shifting, crashing.

On the deserted road home
my children bicycled in front and I followed
with my headlight on their backs:

They glowed in the darkness,
small creatures turning and shifting
and, for a moment, filled with song in the darkness.

II. City

Some are born in their place, some find it,
some realize after long searching that the place they left
is the one they have been searching for.

—Wallace Stegner, "The Sense of Place"

The Problem with Being Born and Raised in Portland

When saliva from the sky slathers my windshield every day
and caraway seeds appear on the sideview mirror,
through the sunroof I rage at the rain
and look upon myself and curse my fate,
wishing balmy skies
or employment in a sunnier state.
Then I swing south, through canyons of clouds,
eucalyptus, stucco, warm smog alluring,
Interstate 5 so easy, LA's a two-day journey.
But the raindrops rust iron resolve;
I retreat, lean back in my seat,
and always return, taciturn,
to the Pendletons and passivity
of Portland.

Once More the Oregon Woods

I have served silicon Rome
tethered to briefcase, terminal, and desk;
I have spoken the universal magnetic tongue
and am glad at last to limp sullenly home.

The night seethes silently through the evergreen trees
near the cabin on the edge of a wood
where quietly I sit amid cedars and sparrows
to watch the wind turn the fallen leaves.

I only vaguely recall the golds and greys
of California sunset on concrete plains,
of afternoons sitting on a Plexiglas saucer
swiveling and scribbling in a binary haze.

For a long time I walked an electronic floor,
pacing a stainless steel cage:
Happy the few ever able to return
to watch moonlight simply filling an open door.

Palmer

Just after 5 o'clock
on what is now the TriMet 51
but then was the Rose City Traction Company
Council Crest,
rain-coated men packed the bus.

The ones I knew were all lawyers.
They loomed large,
rectangular blocks of sandstone and basalt.
They sat in all the back seats
even across the back bench,
where I usually sat.

They held square briefcases on their knees,
as if whenever they got on
the bus developed fold-down trays
of leather-topped desks.

The gruff, remote talk
intended to exclude.
The biggest, gruffest, most towering, was always Bill Palmer,
with wavy white hair,
and white eyebrows which like cumulus clouds
billowed across his forehead.

He seemed never to smile.
But I would stand in front of his house and watch
as he tied the big yellow whitewater raft
to the family station wagon
and packed paddles and bundles of who knows what.
A hush would settle on our street
of towering cedars and firs
as the old oversized rubber raft,
a muted splash of color
patched and smudged,
sat on the car.

Where did he head with his family and raft?
We never knew for sure,
but as I watched, I could smell sage and madrona and alpine soil,
and see Jeffery pines bending in a mountain breeze.

Stroke

So many aunts and uncles and grandparents died—
Uncle George, towering above with bushy white hair,
   who played with us kids,
our favorite grandmother, large and happy,
   who listened to us,

Aunt Alice, thin, a wisp, like a ragged-sailed four-masted
   shipwreck in the surf,
and our other grandmother of endless Sunday dinners,
   who judged everyone.

Then Aunt Willima, gaunt wife of Uncle George,
Aunt Jean, piano teacher to the wealthy children of Dunthorpe,
   and our piano teacher, too,
Uncle Carey, who walked to the store for gum whenever
   we came, happy to hand Wrigley's to any child.

Why had they died, we kids wanted to know.
Always only one answer: "Stroke,"
a word which sent a crease of consternation
across a grown-up's forehead.

Stroke: Swimming through life,
you get into pretty thick water in your eighties,
you lift your arm one last time, and
zap! You're dead.

But first, just robbed of power.
Aunts, uncles, grandparents:
We visited in the hospital or nursing home
while they lay there,
unable to move one whole side,
unable to speak,
tears streaming down their cheeks
while we kids ran around the bed,
examining the drapes, the rugs,
the many curtains hanging mid-room.
For months, we would return every few days or week,
and then—

On Memorial Day we cleaned off bird poop and algae
and laid rhododendrons and roses
on so many River View Cemetery graves.

Walking the Sky

For May Robertson McCracken

In 1917 my grandmother rode into the sky
while walking the lift span of the Hawthorne Bridge.
The Willamette River dropped away from under her,
the wind whipped her dress around her legs,

and she rose to join the gulls circling overhead.
The only pedestrian on the bridge,
saving streetcar fare by walking downtown,
she smiled and waved at the bridge tender above her,

she waved to her children safe at Buckman School,
she waved to her husband at work downtown.
The pulleys turned, and seventeen hundred thousand
pounds of weight sank below her.

As she stood between the two towers high above Portland,
a ship passed under her, loaded maybe with wheat or logs,
and in a few minutes she had descended to a common level.
We call it the day my grandmother walked the sky.

Walking Home from School

Down Patton, where in third grade Hanlon and two others discovered a
    body rolled down the hill into the woods,
to the curve at the house with the doorknob in the middle of the door,
    where my mother's 1950 Chrysler lost its brakes and crashed into a
    car coming uphill, sending my preschool brother into the windshield,
    attended to by the physician driving to work in the car behind her;
past Old English Lane, where my sister's horse-riding friends lived and
    we picked her up after riding lessons at Highland Academy in Sylvan;

under Pat Hodges' house on the hillside, where we always honked,
past the Veazies', with their stone garden wall,
past the house with a basalt stone-walled courtyard;

to Strohecker's playground with its bathroom cottage and Little League
    baseball fields where Tom got a bloody nose playing catcher, the red
    drips matching the red stitching of MAC and the Winged M on his
    uniform;
past Strohecker's Grocery, the only commercial building the whole walk
    home, with gum and candy we never bought;
past the Angells' grandmother's house where a teenager set off a rocket in
    the basement, which shot up through the floors of the house and out the
    attic roof, gathering the whole neighborhood to watch the firefighting;

down Montgomery Drive of concrete slabs,
up steep Isabella Street, the shortest street in the city, to Vista Avenue,
and the curve where once two old women in a 1940s sedan leapt the curb
    and wrestled the car back into the street before hitting us;

and then home territory, Buena Vista Drive, every front door as familiar
    as the doors in our upstairs hallway,
known faces and names and stories behind each:
the coda to a mile-long songline for a ten-year-old
through a storied landscape.

Putt-putt Boats

I like to play indoors better 'cause that's where all the
electrical outlets are. — *A fourth-grader in San Diego,*
quoted in Richard Louv's Last Child in the Woods

We played outdoors with earth, air, fire, and water—
the full range of what could damage and heal.
One June morning after school's end, the white nose of a sprinkler
sniffed our ankles as we cut across the neighbors' steep yard.

Laurel branches grabbed at our shoulders, tugged at our waists
as we pushed through a hedge into the woods, four siblings
with matches and birthday candles
and a fleet of metal putt-putt boats.

We switchbacked up the hillside paths
through hazel and rhododendron to a rocked-in pond.
We set our fleet afloat with birthday candles aflame.
They bratted and brattled across the ten-foot pond.

In the green light under the maples and firs
with knee or foot on a mossy rock and stick in hand,
we leaned over the black water to guide the boats.
Every day we so experienced the world in our flesh:

street gravel embedded in the raw knee,
a gasp for air after too long under an unexpected wave,
a flaming match test-dropped into the empty paint thinner can,
a pocketknife whittle stroke cut to white bone.

Our boats butted opposite shores,
nosed into rocky coves, and nibbled at stone,
exploring the shadows while the heavy overcast
breathed like a giant lung, after school was out.

Streetcar CC 506

Summer evenings we used to crawl into streetcar 506
where it sat brooding on a steep hillside of grass
in Council Crest Park. Older kids
showed how to crawl underneath, push up a floorboard,
and set it aside like a trap door into an attic of heirlooms.

We hoisted ourselves up into a past
that had disappeared before we were born.
We sat in the rigid wicker chairs
with their woody feel and antique look
of the woven hats of old men.

We stood at the controls and touched every brass bar and knob.
We ran the streetcar in our imaginations down precipitous streets,
clanging at every curve. We passed the Fountain,
swung wide on Ravensview over the city,
turned at Ainsworth School and zoomed down Vista.

Years later, I zoomed my father's 1964 Chrysler New Yorker
down that same steep streetcar route a rainy high school gameday,
passing the slowpokes until the car started spinning.
We hit a guardrail going backwards. In the sudden silence,
Bill Murphy in the passenger seat asked, "Want a sandwich?"

Late that evening, as I explained, the spilled gasoline of my story
trickled closer and closer to the burning flare of my father's anger.
But finally he said only, "I hope it was worth it," and then, "Good night."
The conductor waved, the bell clanged, and I took that streetcar
again through the soft summer night, and all the city lights below
   winked.

Google Maps: Biking Buena Vista Drive

I click the mouse and
my childhood Portland street appears,
bathed in late-summer sunshine!

The arrow leads me on the route
I bicycled endlessly the years
I was seven and eight and nine years old.

Past the doors of the Shroeders,
the Palmers, the Otises, the Langfitts,
the Dryers, the Robertsons—

on up to make the turn at Vista,
and coast back down again and further,
past the Monroes, the Bushes, the DeFrances, the Savinars—

as if a lifetime hadn't occurred,
and it's again 1958—
there's a new saddle to see in the Dryers' basement,

and the Angells just got Sparky,
who would never bite anyone,
and we stop our backyard game to watch a jet plane.

Down the backside, along Montgomery Street,
I pause the mouse at the new wrought-iron gates
leading up steps to backyards.

The grillwork and thimbleberries say
Slow down and study me,
which I still do, as any seven-year old would.

Not Gophers, but Moles: Portland Backyards before the Days of ChemLawn

These days our neighbors' flawless lawns
wear the richest coats of the deepest green
thanks to heavy doses of phosphorus, potassium, and nitrogen.

Long ago we played from spring through fall in backyards
bristling with dandelions, clover, and plantain
which stayed green without watering or summer rain.

The sudden new molehills were always a wonder:
furry animals lived underground,
sharing our yard upside down.

But the little brown shield volcanoes
made badminton difficult,
so like the scientists on TV, we did our experiments.

We pulled away the dirt and stuck in a hose,
and watered, and watered, and watered.
the ground took all we offered.

We tossed in lit firecrackers, and covered the hole,
then ran to other hills, pulled away dirt,
and saw only smoke rise skyward.

We leveled the hills with the push mower,
but always they multiplied.
Three feet away, like bread, again more would rise.

By summer's end and into fall
our well-used yard of scuffed-bare spots
sported its own coat of little brown hill polka-dots.

December Wind

For three days the east wind has blown
in the fir trees, the cedars, and the ash.
It sounds like freeway traffic accelerating.

Leaves and needles pelt the windows at 2 a.m.,
an impatient friend
calling us to adventure,
who we ignore.

Sometimes the wind roars and subsides,
roars and subsides, faster and faster:
We are protons in a cyclotron.
We long to be swept away.

Now just before dawn, just above freezing
the beams of our house creak
as on a too sunny day
and we wake to common breakfast.

January Lessons

Portlanders learn to conjugate
fog, mist, drizzle, shower—
amo, amas, amat:
It's why our skin is so soft, our hair so supple.

After weeks of warm west rain, an east wind
roars down the gorge,
topples the cottonwood across Ash Creek,
drops the easy-living fir down the street.

When Portland clay sloughs off hillsides,
hundred-foot Douglas firs
take a downhill ride
turning Montgomery Street into Walking Woods Drive.

When mudslides block Cardinell Terrace
and retaining walls sigh in a burst of basalt stones,
then we know it's January,
and winter's placed its wet stamp on Portland.

Ice Storm Paralyzes City

Poets hope for extremes in weather—
it's part of the job.
Sure, sure, antennae of the race,
speaking the eternal verities,
poets yearn for spring,

but spring comes too soon and too easily.
Daffodils now in February,
and Portland still hasn't had a big snow,
a big freeze and silver thaw.
We haven't yet known we're alive

by seeing the world's heart stop:
the crack and whoosh of a fallen branch
too loaded with ice to hold,
the rifle-shot cry of wood too cold
to stay silent—

We hope for the brittle hard world of legendary winter
to stop commerce and the quotidian
and in the deathly tranquil city to tell us:
Look at your breath: You, are, alive.
Look at how little you need to survive.

Morning Project

I've taken a chorus
of daffodils,
trimmed their frills,
and laid the petals end to end—
liferafts on a kitchen-table sea.

And on every canary's wing of them
I've penned a measure
of the polyphonies of spring.

Out the window and into the gray-blue air
my foolscap liferafts
catch on updrafts
and clobber the bent-headed
work-oriented
professionals
scurrying to desk and chair.

Sitting in suit on sidewalk and swearing,
suddenly one sees—
a towhee,
a worm,
and then the whole winter
evaporates
on a robin-filled breeze.

Folding Laundry

My son's tie-dye t-shirt from Outdoor School
explodes color bombs from sixth grade.

His pale blue polo shirt from the Oregon Zoo
is a piece of early-summer-morning sky.

My daughter's red lifeguard shirt
puddles into a pool of dried blood.

I fold the shirts face down in thirds, then thirds again,
and flip them over. We stare at each other.

I carefully place the stacks into their laundry baskets
like putting bones and fingernails and hair into reliquaries,

every item of my children precious
in this unpredictable world.

Night Moose

"I'm sorry," I tell my three-year-old,
"but I've put the moose pepper down
three times already.
I don't think a moose will break into your room tonight."

It's 3:21 a.m. and
the train whistles and horns
in the Tigard switching yards
two miles away
drift through my son's windows.

His small body hunches on his bed,
chest to pillow,
buttocks in the air,
a giant frog.
"That's just a train," I tell him.

"No," he insists. "I heard a moose outside.
Did you hear it?
There it is again.
Will it come here?"

I shake the pepper cellar along the window,
the closet doors,
the hall door,
the bed.

I open the shade a few inches, and see
our yard and street
alive and crawling
with cougars,
and wolves,
and moose.

Lucky Day, after Petroleum

This could be your lucky day—
the day you lose your comfort
and learn where you live.

This could be your jackpot day—
the day we demand too much,
and forever lose the power grid.

What is a computer, but a handful of sand?
Plastic and sand, says the CIO.
Systems may fail and hard drives crash,
but ink and paper abide.

This could be our lucky day—
the day our cars don't start,
the freeway quiets like a mountain meadow,

and we stare in wonder at dew on the grass,
fog lifts off the river,
and our neighbors turn from their screens
and come out to blink in the sunlight.

Walking to Work

I pass the creek next to our house.
Winter it's a stairway of waterfalls,
but now in early fall, before the rains begin,
its dozens of eyes stare unblinking at the sky.

My son is a stone staircase of Columbia River basalt
as finely joined as Italian masons ever managed,
flight after flight rising under a canopy of bigleaf maples,
solid, fixed in place, waiting for venturous walkers.

As I walk up the slopes of Mount Sylvania,
cars pull cautiously out of side streets, pause,
and race through the trees to the highway,
fox squirrels and leaves tumbling in their backwash.

My daughter is a snow-capped peak
with the new-risen sun on its shoulder.
She smiles and ice crystals sparkle.
The alpine tarns absorb all light.

I walk in mud through the woods.
Small animals hatch along the edges of my shoes
and make snappy little comments about
my speed, my agility, and the weather.

Beside the path, flickers hammer the dead trees,
scarves of fog weave through the scraggly third-growth.
I step out of the woods, cross the perimeter road,
and begin the acres of asphalt to my office.

Soon I will stand before a whiteboard,
dozens of eyes unblinking upon me,
and hammer my head against student
paragraphs dense as basalt, sentences like roadkill.

III. Mountains

Montani semper liberi.

Mountaineers are always freemen.

The Passionate Hiker to His Love

Come hike with me and be my love
and you will know the trails of Oxbow Park
waterproof, windproof, and breathable.

For I have bought you a Gore-Tex parka
of a thousand threads per inch:
They susurrate like wind in Sitka spruce.

A drawcord waist and ripstop fabric
and easy-opening underarm vents:
If these pleasures may thee move,
come hike with me and be my love.

Who has patience has all things:
L. L. Bean ships the 17th.
Till then live with me and I will be
your waterproof, windproof, whispering love.

Birthday Hike

February, Multnomah-Wahkeena Loop

Like few others this stormy day
I leave solidity behind and
start the trail upwards into fog.

On snow bridges over creeks
I expect to fall through to
a hidden world of hope.

Asterisks of snow fly at each footfall
on the slog upslope amid
parentheses of hemlock needles.

I read my life in scree
slope, snow field, mosspatch:
what's behind similar to what's ahead.

In the quiet my breath steamwhistles visible puffs
at four hundred, eight hundred, twelve hundred feet
till the trail levels into a carpet of green needles,

cushioned and colorful and
leading me straight to the bright white
chaos and roar of life at Wahkeena Falls.

The Glaciers Are Leaving Us

Mt. Hood

As a treat for days on the trail
we stopped at Timberline Lodge
and stared appalled
at Palmer Snowfield—

A suggestion of snow and ice
against the hot dry rocks of Mt. Hood
above the lodge,
like a cloud against the sand.

Summers past we've watched snowboarders and skiers
like tiny drops of liquid
trickle down the square patch of groomed snow on the glacial ice
and return to the lodge in a ravine of snow.

And now: The glaciers are leaving us—
only a smidgeon of dirty, abandoned ice,
high, and higher up,
the ravine of connecting snow long melted.

Memaloose Lake

Clackamas Foothills

In the photo, Andrew stands by the car,
backpack frame like a saintly aureole
rising above his nine-year-old head.

Beneath his visored hat,
he grins as wide as the mountain hemlocks are green
on this first day of the first backpack of his life.

Thermometer and compass on a green lanyard
dangle data for the right decisions.
His "Cub World" t-shirt reminds of sanitized Scout campouts.
Now we're on steeper slopes, where the rules
of common sense and nature prevail.

A clearcut mountain suns behind my son.
We're about to enter the woods on the left
filled with shadows and a few spots of light
on our long trip to Memaloose Lake.

On the Timberline Trail

Mt. Hood Wilderness

Elk Cove gives us April and May in August:
this north side of the mountain
goes backwards in time from the valleys below

where our lawn has been brown for a month,
our rhododendrons stressed in the afternoon sun,
the clay soil as dry and hard as a kiln-bisqued pot.

But in this high basin the creeks race
glacial-melt chocolate brown
and wildflowers nod approval of mile-high views.

Creekside monkeyflowers wave pink and yellow,
avalanche lilies across the meadows hang demure heads:
We have it good here, they know.

Lupine, paintbrush, gentian—the flowers soak up the colors
and concentrate them into a thousand
spots of pink, red, purple, blue, yellow, and white.

The evening's alpenglow makes magic all who watch
mountain snow turn pink
and radiate color long after sunset.

After breakfast we hike higher up a creek for clear water,
and cool off in the gaping mouth of an ice cave.
We are in Oz, Narnia, Neverland, Middle Earth.

On our hike out not even the ice water
of Coe and Compass creeks
can wash the magic from our feet.

Perseid Meteor Shower

Mt. Hood Wilderness

My daughter and I roll out sleeping bags
onto our moss-green tarp
on this ridgeline above Cast Lake.

Here, far from city lights, almost a mile up,
the stars shyly hint their presence
in the sundown sky.

Alpine hemlocks and firs crowd the sky
but minute by minute more stars
arrive and take their seats for the evening.

We wait and wait, the temperature dropping,
the wind hurdling the ridge like a track star,
animals quieting for the Main Event.

A streak of light zips across the sky!
But the firmament makes no sound, offers no applause.
"Did you see that!" Julia shouts in admiration.

We wait and watch, a quick line here, a hint there.
The shooting stars perform against a not-quite-yet-black scrim,
warming up for the sixty-per-hour show.

But then the unwelcome moon glows behind a ridge
and rises, blotting the stars with chalk-white light—
jealous celebrity, night sky heavyweight.

Obsidian Falls

Three Sisters Wilderness

Walking the Obsidian Trail is like walking a kitchen floor
after the earthquake has emptied the cabinets:
crunch, crunch, crunch.

The trail sparkles as if for millennia the deer and elk
have tossed their beer bottles over the cliffs,
shards embedding in dirt.

Such a mess—broken glass everywhere,
black that flashes bright in the sunlight,
black that brightens the lupine and paintbrush meadows.

My daughter and I crush and scatter the obsidian chips,
sparkling and shining,
as we walk along the mile-high black-glass trail.

Our comments domesticate the wilderness to make it ours,
to make it our home
from which we've been away too long.

Sometimes we hear the sound of boot on fresh snowfall
when the temperature's below freezing,
a muffled crunch in the quiet of an overcast day.

Sometimes we hear the brittle rattle of thin sharp glass underfoot,
like when you wonder how you could have dropped the vase,
prelude to dustpan and broom.

Sometimes we hear the clinking of marbles shot across a rug,
dice in a cup,
a handful of poker chips dropped on the table.

When we stop, in the silence we hear the rockfall
of knapped arrowheads and knifeblades
which slid for centuries from this cutlery to all points of the compass.

Julia at Lost Lake

Mt. Hood National Forest

She cups blueberries in her hand
as if they were a broken-winged bird
which she eats morsel by morsel.

Long coils of her light-brown hair
twist and curl down her shoulder,
across the orange life vest tied loosely in front.

Ten years old, she's comfortable and confident
standing above the Old Town canoe beached by the blueberries
in the volcanic gravel of the far shore.

At her bare feet in the water
blue dragonflies, rough-skinned newts,
kokanee probe and vanish.

Alder and devil's club crowd the shore at her shoulder.
In the distance ghost trees here and there whiten
the dense green hemlock August.

From her own palm she plucks and tastes the world
and then shakes remnant leaves and stems like confetti
and climbs in to fly across white caps and swells to the waiting dock.

At the I-84 Rest Area

Memaloose,
island of the dead,
lies like a vandalized tombstone
on the green lawn of the Columbia.

Downriver, Bonneville Dam
tells the Columbia when to roll on,
when to wait.

Once the terminus of the Oregon Trail,
the river here roared
as it rushed a rocky channel,
two hundred yards
white as a field of snow.

The dams—
Bonneville, The Dalles, John Day, McNary—
do the talking today.

The river turns a deeper green
under an August breeze.
Memaloose, island of the dead,
shines as pleasantly as a concrete sidewalk
in a city park.

The Columbia lies quietly
atop the former rapids,
atop the shouting snowfield,
as dishonestly beautiful as dichondra.

One Track

The mind is the back side of a waterfall,
hard basalt,
slippery and slick,
protected,
enjoying a good view through the
razzle-dazzle of the busy waters,
itself unmoved.

The mind is the yellow skunk cabbage in early spring
poking through the swampiest, most unstable ground,
brilliant, glowing against the muck,
a lone thick bulbous candle
in a caul of shimmering incandescent light.

The mind is the wind
in the cottonwoods and alders along the creek,
filling the silence with chatter and sudden gusts,
worrying the leaves
and fiddling with every catkin and cone.

The mind is a pet rat,
chewing through obstacles,
stealing keys and gum wrappers and buttons,
fixated on whatever presents itself,
scurrying in darkness along the safety of a fixed wall
and then unpredictably leaping through the air, acrobatic,
and pausing to lick itself clean.

About the Author

Michael McDowell has published fiction, poetry, and nonfiction in such publications as *Penny Dreadful, Pawn Review,* and *South Carolina Review*. He currently writes prose mostly about nature and landscape writing and poetry mostly about "a sense of place." Some of the prose appears in the anthologies *The Ecocriticism Reader* (University of Georgia Press, 1996), *Reading the Earth* (University of Idaho Press, 1998), and *Fifty Key Thinkers on the Environment* (Routledge, 2001). Some of the poetry appears in *Windfall: A Journal of Poetry of Place,* which he co-edits with Bill Siverly. He has an AB from Stanford University, an MA from the University of Virginia, and a PhD from the University of Oregon. He lives in Portland, Oregon, where he teaches literature and writing at Portland Community College.

About Windfall Press

Besides publishing books of high quality poetry, Windfall Press also publishes *Windfall: A Journal of Poetry of Place. Windfall* features poetry which captures the spirit of place as part of the essence of the poem, particularly poetry of the Pacific Northwest which is attentive to the relationships between people and the landscapes in which we live.

Colophon

The text is set in Palatino, which was designed by Hermann Zapf and initially released in 1948 by the Linotype foundry. The titles are set in Bodoni, a typeface designed by Giambattista Bodoni in 1790 and updated in 1926 by Heinrich Jost.